ELLEN JOHNSON

A LITTLE DREAMING

BY
FENTON JOHNSON

McGrath Publishing Company
College Park, Maryland

Reprint McGrath Publishing Company 1969

Library of Congress Catalog Card Number: 73-76113

Manufactured in the United States of America
by Arno Press, Inc., New York

COPYRIGHT 1913
FENTON JOHNSON

TO MY GRANDMOTHER

ELLEN JOHNSON

WHOSE LIFE WAS A POEM FULL OF TENDER SYMPATHY
AND WHOLESOME STRIVING.

Foreword

I, the poor minstrel, wandering through the maze of time, come to thy palace, O my King the Reader, with naught save my little lyre upon which I play my feeble strain. The Gods grant that my songs may please thee and give thee cheer and sympathy for my people.

THE SINGER.

A LITTLE DREAMING

Dream of a Whisper

I

I shall dream!—shall dream
  Of a whisper soft
From the lips divine,
  From the lips aloft,
From the lips of Circe.

II

And my soul awakes,
  Though my eyes are closed;
Pleasure fills my veins,
  As when Venus rose
Sea-nymphs laughed so softly.

III

Fair enchantress, weave,
  Weave a dream for me;
Let my Hellas live
  Down beside the sea—
Sea of starlit strangeness.

The All-time

I

God is in the morning,
God is in the dawning,
God is in the All-time.

II

Morning lark is singing,
Heaven's harp is ringing,
God is in the All-time.

III

Baby's cheeks are dimpling,
Baby's laugh is rippling,
God is in the All-time.

IV

Lonely maid is sighing,
For her lover dying,
God is in the All-time.

V

Autumn leaves are dancing,
In the zephyrs prancing,
God is in the All-time.

VI

God is in the infant's creeping,
God is in the old man's sleeping,
God is in the All-time.

Dunbar

I

Bring me southern cypress,
Bring me weeping willow,
Let me mourn for Dunbar—
Bard of happiness.

II

Never shall a singing,
Of old passions clinging,
Come forth as from Dunbar—
Bard of grief and woe.

III

Joys of mirth and sorrow
Have been sung in accents
From the soul of Dunbar—
Bard of everything.

Beloved

I

Fair Lucille, my love is warm
As the honey-bees that swarm
In the June-time, happy time,
In the June-time, summer's prime;
Oh, my love is sweetly rare,
Like the breeze of evening air,
And a crystal touch from thee
Brings fresh zephyrs from the sea.

II

Love may come and love may go,
Like the winter's drifting snow;
Love may wither, shrink, and die,
Like the maize in hot July;
But my soul shall cherish one
With the fervor of the sun;
And, no matter what I feel,
I shall always love Lucille.

What Mistah Robin Sais

I

In de shady wood de weathah's cool,
Down beside ole Massa Ketchum's pool;
Dah Ah sits me 'pon de mossy logs,
Talkin' wid de hoppin' buhds an' frogs,
List'nin' to dey singin' an' dey noise,—
Happy kase it brings a thousan' joys.
Mistah Robin sais, "You nevah min'—
Striped am de watahmelyon rin';
Moistens all yo' insides, froo an' froo;
So you shouldn't 'peah so down an' blue."

II

Wondah if in haiven dey's a wood?
Wondah if 'twas dah mah mammy stood
When mah po' ole daddy piked away?
Wondah if de robins sing up daih,
An' de froggies, in dey coat o' green,
Wid de fluhtin' shaddahs may be seen?
Mistah Robin sais, "You nevah min'—
Striped am de watahmelyon rin';
Moistens all yo' insides, froo an' froo;
So you shouldn't 'peah so down an' blue."

Love's Good-Night

I

Good-night! Good-night! My love, good-
    night!
We shall meet here again when bright
The moon shines o'er the distant hill,
And mocking-bird begins to trill.

II

What though a parent's wrath should come?
It cannot make my loving dumb;
To-morrow night I shall await
You here, at our love's trysting-gate.

III

And in the days that shall be here,
Your love my full soul shall revere;
So, till the rounded moon comes bright,
Good-night! My love, good-night! Good-
    night!

Swinburne

I

Weep, ye Western isle! Swinburne is dead;
Far across the vale his soul has fled
To the shadow-land, the land of rest,
Where the poets sleep on Homer's breast.
Carve the myrtle with a gleaming pen
From the quill of robin or of wren,
For the night has come upon the land,—
Oh, the night has come upon the land!

II

In the yesterdays we saw the light
At a distance in the mystic night;
In the yesterdays the Muse came down
And in fire she painted Nature's sound;
But to-day the world's dull hour is here,
While old England crowds around the bier
Of the last of all the songster tribe,—
Last unloved of all the songster tribe.

III

Angels weave a crown of evergreen,
In the land no mortal eye has seen;
And, when stars are singing in the blue,

And the downy clouds are changing hue,
These white souls will deck their brother's
 brow,
And in reverence their heads will bow
To the sweet-voiced singer of the West,—
Last sweet-voicéd singer of the West.

Launcelot's Defiance

My liege the King, why burns the flame of
 wrath
Upon thy cheek? Is it for Guinevere?
Ah, well, sweet lord, I know that she is
 Queen
Of Britain and of towered Camelot;
But I am king of all the mettled knights
Who sit at Arthur's board when wine is red.
No, Arthur! sheathe thy sword! Excalibir
Is naught beside the wrath of Launcelot;
For I can pierce the sun, the stars, the moon,
And fiends of Hell do crouch with limping
 fear
When I am clothed in dark displeasure's
 robes.
The right is mine and I will draw my blade
Into the breach! For Christ and Guinevere!

Uncle Isham Lies a-Dyin'

Oh, de dahk an' dreahy night am camein,
Thru de cabin do' de night am camein';
All alone yo' Uncle Isham lies,
An' de def-lights shinin' in his eyes.
Chillun done fo'sook me good an' clean;
Lef' me 'out a strip o' bacon skin;
Took all dat Ah had, an' went up nofe,
Whah dey's nuffin' 'tall to do but loaf,
While dey Uncle Isham lies a-dyin',
Po' ole Uncle Isham lies a-dyin'.

II

What! am dat yo' flittin' 'round, mah
    Mandy?
Flittin' 'round in robes o' white, mah
    Mandy?
Po' ole Isham's on his lastes' now;
Kain't go out no mo' to hoe an' plow;
Gwine to jine de hebben ban' wid you;
Gwine to be whar skies am allus blue,
An' de Rivah Johdan's flowin' free
Down to hebben's big and mighty sea;
An' de chillun lose dey monstrus
    meanness,—
Heahtless chillun lose dey monstrus
    meanness.

15

Gift o' Love to Me

I

I was a very lonely lad,
  I was a lad without a hope;
I was a lad who fought the world,
  The king, the tyrant, and the Pope.
I was a lad who had a soul,
  And many thousand ills could feel,—
Until the walls of stone fell down,
  And God, dear God, sent me Lucille.

II

I wandered in the darkness drear,
  Along the curvéd country path;
I shuddered at each little sound,
  Like man when God is in His wrath.
The years had claimed their toll of pain,
  The wounds of childhood would not
        heal;
I would have died in Sorrow's arms,—
  But God, dear God, sent me Lucille.

III

And now at eve I pray to Him,
  And find His face in every star;
His tender mercy has no end,
  His guiding light shines from afar.

And when the moon is full and round,
　　Before His presence do I kneel;
For I can read from out my heart
　　That God, dear God, sent me Lucille.

Waters of Forgetfulness

Waters of forgetfulness,
Waters of the River Lethe,
Bearing on thy gentle waves
Souls of those who passed beyond;
Let me drink but one small drop,
Let my sorrows pass away,
Pass away and be no more;
Let my yearning cease and die,
Like the beating of a heart
When the Angel Death has come,
Ruthless, at the chamber door.
As the Trojan, homeward bound,
Saw the light above the Styx,
So my heart is glad when morn
Has descended straight to me.
Waters of forgetfulness,
Waters of the River Lethe,
Let me drink but one small drop,—
Then shall I have joy and peace.

Kentucky Moon

I

Kentucky moon outshines my sweetheart's
    eye,
        Lullabye, lullabye;
Kentucky moon, for you each night I sigh,
        Lullabye, lullabye;
Upon my love you shed your silver stream,
When she is veiled in midnight's mystic
    dream;
You kiss her brow and give her peace and
    rest,
And ever wish our troth were amply blest;
        Lullabye, lullabye.

II

Kentucky moon, for you the blue-grass
    grows,
        Lullabye, lullabye;
Kentucky moon, for you Ohio flows,
        Lullabye, lullabye;
The black man looks from out his cabin door
To where your wingéd rays forever soar,
And deep within his heart he prays that you
Might ever grace the dark and silent blue;
        Lullabye, lullabye.

The Plaint of the Factory Child

I

Mother, must I work all day?
All the day? Ay, all the day?
Must my little hands be torn?
And my heart bleed, all forlorn?
I am but a child of five,
And the street is all alive
With the tops and balls and toys,—
Pretty tops and balls and toys.

II

Day in, day out, I toil—toil!
And all that I know is toil;
Never laugh as others do,
Never cry as others do,
Never see the stars at night,
Nor the golden glow of sunlight,—
And all for but a silver coin,—
Just a worthless silver coin.

III

Would that death might come to me!
That blessed death might come to me,
And lead me to waters cool,
Lying in a tranquil pool,

Up there where the angels sing,
And the ivy tendrils cling
To the land of play and song,—
Fairy land of play and song.

Death of Love

I

Where sinks deep my love, dead love,
That so warmly glowed awhile?
Where the passion of my dreams
And the kiss of afterwhile?
In the City of Delight,
In the palace built of air,
In the smile of dying Day
And the vision of Despair.

II

Not where Morning shakes the dew
From the sunshine of her locks;
Not where Evening breathes her flame
And the moon so gently rocks;
But where gleams the firefly's wing
In the swamp of dead desire;
And a fairy shrinks amazed
At the passing of the fire.

Down Upon the Palatine

I

Once there stood beside the Rhine,—
Down beside the German Rhine,
Where the vines of grapes entwine,
And the vats are full of wine,—
Uhlfrid's castle, ancient mart
Of the noble and the grand,
In the great, romantic land
That we call the Palatine.

II

There the lovers sighed and sighed,
There the nobles drunk with pride,
Fought all night and fought all day,
And ne'er deemed it aught but play;
There the troubadours with song
Charmed the merry all night long;
There the knights rescued the weak;
There the priests were low and meek,—
Down upon the Palatine.

III

Oh, were I beside the Rhine,—
Down beside the German Rhine,—
All the day in happiness

Would my soul and I be blest!
And I would dream of that fair past,
And the richly sweet contrast
Of the red against the blue,
And a moonlight night with you,
Down upon the Palatine.

Flower of the Summer Night

Flower of the summer night,
Picture of the pale moonlight,
Love of youth, eternal love,
Borne from angels up above.
Night and day I sing a song
Of thee, my pretty, rosy Dawn;
And the sorrows and the pain
Live within my soul again.
Oh, to look into thy heart,
And find there sweet Cupid's part!
Such a joy no angel knows,
In the land where Jordan flows;
But the fate of love is fate,
Come it early, come it late,
So my lyre shall sing of her
With the songs that passion stir.

Rome Is Dying

I

Rome is dying,—
Rome the Mighty!—
The sea of gold engulfs her form,
And men are buying fellow-men.
The tide of prejudice rolls on
Beyond the Tiber, dark and cold;
The prophet sees the fading light,
And shudders at the growing night.
The land is red with crying blood;
The people murmur and are hushed.
Rome is dying,—
Rome the Mighty!

II

Rome is dying,—
Rome the Mighty!
And what the sinner sows, he reaps.
Ye made our women slaves and dogs;
The serpent lash was yours to wield,
O boastful Mother of the West!
Ye nurtured strangers in the land,—
A mongrel breed of humankind;

Ye made them grind the ripened corn
To feed patricians born to scorn.
Rome is dying,—
Rome the Mighty!

III

Rome is dying,—
Rome the Mighty!—
Who used the common tyrant clay
To mold a consul with the mermaid
    smile.
Rome passes down to Pluto's realm
With boasts that shock old Cicero;
She lauds the painted woman form
That sits and spins the roulette wheel;
She shouts to see her Crassus rise
On the toil-stained frames of men.
Rome is dying,—
Rome the Mighty!

Ruby

I

Dream of a sapphire,
Dream of youth's empire,
  In a crimson stone;
Beauty rare sparkling,
Laughter deep startling
  In a silver tone.

II

Soul of a day-dream,
Soul of a sunbeam,
  In its liveliness;
Soul of the dreary,
Soul of the weary,
  In its loneliness.

III

Like a sweet singing
Is the clear ringing
  Of her happy voice;
Full of the pleasure,
Full of the treasure
  That gives life its joys.

IV

Let us be drinking
With the glass clinking
   To the charming name;
Let us lose trouble
In life's sweet bubble
   And fair Ruby's fame.

Where Is Fame?

I

"Where is Fame?" the dreamer asked,
"Where is gilded wingéd Fame?"
"In the land of dreams and sighs,
O'er the sea of bitter woe,
Where the burnished moon is dark
And the moans are never hushed,
In the desert of Nowhere,
Where the dead men grin all night
And the ghosts of camels whine,
Down by yonder row of graves,
Ever yawning for its food
Flies my gilded wingéd Fame."

The Lover's Soliloquy

I

Love's charm belongs to every age and
    clime;
To every sep'rate man the burning flame
Comes once or twice or thrice, as wills the
    God.
In Ethiop, beneath the rose-dipped sun,
My fathers wooed their dusky paramours,
As you and I, in this, our latter day;
And where the silver-breast Euphrates lies,
A mirror for the milk-white moon to shine,
Our common parent sighed for Mother Eve.
As you and I, in this, our latter day

II

Without the passion love, no sun would
    glow,
No golden moon would grace the summer
    eve;
The golden-rod would cease to charm the
    eye;
The gilded rose would wither ere its day,
And all the general universe be black;

For when within thy heart thou know'st
that Love
Hath wrought his miracle, thou art a God,
And all that is of earth is slave to thee.

May

Come out, you buds, that sleep!
The year's glad time is here.
Rejoice with everyone;
The rivers dance with joy.
The gleam is on the boy
Who hears the grasses sing
This song of jubilee:
"Sweet May, sweet May is here—
The lovely May is here."

Mistah Witch

Say, who's dat a-comin' now?
Mistah Witch, Mistah Witch;
Jumpin' high from bough to bough,
Mistah Witch, Mistah Witch.
Ain't you tiahed o' skeahin' me,
Mistah Witch, Mistah Witch?
Wid yo' eyes lak hellish sea,
Mistah Witch, Mistah Witch.

My Love*

I

Young gallant from the fairer race of men,
  Have you a love as comely as the maid
To whom I chant my lyre-strung passion
      songs?
  Has she large eyes that gleam from out
    the shade,
And voice as low as when Ohio stream
Glides silently along a summer dream?

II

Her face is golden, like the setting sun,
  Her teeth as white as winter's virgin
      snow;
Her smile is like a gleam from Paradise,
  Her laugh the sweetest music that I know;
And all the wide, wide world is but a mite,
When she, my darling elf, is in my sight.

III

Let Sorrow wring the blood from out my
      heart,
  Let Melancholy be my daily book,
Let all the earth be like a sinner's grave,
  And let my wand'ring spirit never look
Upon the kingdom, if my damozel
From out my soul the charm of love dispel.

* Published in THE CRISIS, New York.

In de Beulahlan'

I

Def am but a sleepin'
Def am but a creepin'
  From de Shaddahlan';
Dah mah mammy's standin'
On de golden landin'
  Ob de Beulahlan'.

II

All de dahkies shoutin',
Satan goes a-crouchin',
  In de Shaddahlan';
Mandy's robes am swayin',
On a hahp she's playin',
  In de Beulahlan'.

III

Now she's white ez jaspuh;
Wish dat Ah could clasp huh
  In de Shaddahlan';
"Honey mine," she's singin',
To mah name she's clingin'
  In de Beulahlan'.

IV

Heah huh wings a-flappin,
Feathuhs saft ez satin,
  In de Shaddahlan';
Mandy, Ah'se a-camein',
Don yo' brightes' raiment,
  In de Beulahlan'.

Farewell to Lucille

Farewell, Lucille! Love never dies,
  But lingers till the end of time.
From Homer's day, the race of bards
  Sang songs of thee in dainty rhyme;
And I, the humblest of the lot,
  Made thee my goddess and my muse.
Fair Helen's lips were naught to thine;
  Appelles would thy face peruse,
And in a rapture fine paint thee,
  The deity of art and love and grace.
But thou hast chosen from the flowers
  That bloom along this garden-place;
And I am cast aside to die.
  Farewell, Lucille! Farewell! Farewell!

When I Reach Manhood

I

I have never lost the crimson joy
  Of communion with the things of earth.
To-day roses have the rare sweet life
  Of the great celestial dream-birth;
I go down to where the river flows,
  And on soft green grass I lie and talk
With the spirits of the world around;
  And with merry sunbeams do I walk,
As when but a child I walked,—
  The same as when but a laughing child.

II

And when years have changed my hair to
      white,
  Roses will be sweeter far than now;
Time will never dim the mystery
  Of a blossom in its summer glow.
Sympathy is quality of man
  When the twilight ushers in the hour
Of the withered limb and faded eye,
  And the loss of every kind of power;
Soft the world of nature drinks it all,—
  Wonder-world of nature drinks it all.

And the Wound Is Not for Man to See

I

Oh, the pangs of love, the cruel love,
That at morning-time is seen to creep
Stealthily into the victim's heart!
No new-born joy it brings to me,
Nor flowers of May, nor sweet song-time,
From an empty world and a vale of naught;
And who, when the evening-time has come,
Soars to other realms, and leaves the soul
To the tears and anguish of the night,—
To the moanings of the sorrow night,—
Pierce on! I am brave and I am strong,
And the wound is not for man to see.

II

In the solitude I sit and dream
Of a night that passed into the day
When I knew the hour of joy had come
And the June-time was not far away.
She was she, and all the world was naught,
As I read the story of her gentle soul
In the eyes of gray that looked on me.
But the time has changed! Her love is cold,
Like the snows upon the heights

Of icy Switzerland,—the land of frost,—
While this bourne of life is dark and void;
And the wound is not for man to see.

III

Now at noontime, when the sun is high,
And the earth is clothed in gayety,
Ever flitting on, the butterfly,
With his wings of gaudy hue and stripes,
Sips the honey from the rosebud's lips,
And the lily-cup is his as long
As the song of flattery he sings;
But at twilight, homeward goes this swain,
And the lily drops her fairy head,
While the perfumed rosebud sighs for him
As I sigh for her who is no more;
And the wound is not for man to see.

IV

Oh, the tears that Love exacts from all!
Oh, the tears that fall and ever fall,
Would fill the seas in all the lands,
While the rogue is laughing merrily.
Oh, the hearts that lie along the shore!
Broken, torn, and bleeding handiwork
Of the God that made all perfect things;

They are remnants of the summer hour,
Of the moonlight night, and stars sublime;
They are legion, and are everywhere,
With the legend written in red blood:
"And the wound is not for man to see."

Can You Tell Me?

I

Can you tell me where my lover lies,—
Where my thrice-kissed darling lover lies?
Down in Cuba, under starlit skies,
Where the ocean zephyr softly sighs,
And the palm leaves drink the pale
    moonshine,—
Sleeps in shroud of blue, your dear ensign,—
Sleeps for aye and aye your fond ensign.

II

Can you tell me if my lover sighs,—
If for me my darling lover sighs?
In his dreams—his sweet death-dreams—his
    eyes
Wander down to where a maiden's cries
Rend the stillness of the ancient night,
And he longs to be by Cora's side,—
Longs to be by lovesick Cora's side?

The Gleeman's Melody

I

Come, my gleeman, with your melody,
    Angel melody!
Weave from starlight songs of tenderness,
    Songs of tenderness!
Down beneath the curvéd jasper moon,
Down beneath the sea-green ocean croon,
Drop, drop, drop your azure melody,
    Azure melody!

II

From the sea there sparkles melody,
    Coral melody!
Arthur's maidens stop and listen long,
    Stop and listen long!
Fifty fathoms down a minstrel lies,
Fifty fathoms down they hear his cries;
"Jesu!" sing they, " 'Tis a crystal melody,
    Crystal melody!"

III

And the lily croons a melody,
    Golden melody!
O'er the gleeman whom she loved and lost,
    Ay, she loved and lost!

36

Fifty breakers join the ocean choir,
Fifty fairies string the minstrel's lyre;
All the world is like a living melody,
    Living melody!

The Ethiopian s Song

I

Where I go the lily blooms,
Where I go the ivy climbs;
All the earth is slave to me,
All the orbs are merry chimes.
White man longs to rule the world;
I am happy where I am,—
I, the Lord of sweet content.

II

Where I go magnolias dance,
Where I go the jonquils prance;
Strength and might and power
    are mine,
Song and cheer my freedom's lance.
Let Ambition die her death;
I am happy where I am,—
I, the Lord of sweet content.

Down to Eldorado

I

Down to Eldorado, Love,
  Eldorado, land of song,
Where the canopy of red
  In the dying day is hung;
Where the chill of summer sea
Brings a joy to you and me,—
  Down at fairy Eldorado.

II

Down to Eldorado, Love,
  On a palfrey, white as snow;
Up a chiseled mountain steep,
  On a palfrey we shall go;
And our lips the dew shall drink
On the silver river's brink,—
  Down at rosy Eldorado.

III

Down to Eldorado, Love,
  Where the crimson songsters sing;
From the green, green bough at noon,
  Notes of crimson songsters ring,
And the land is full of joy,
Like a happy, year-old boy,—
  Down at golden Eldorado.

IV

Down to Eldorado, Love,
  Over steeple, over spire;
In the darkness of the night,
  Hangs the moon and all its fire;
And two hearts are wildly glad,
And two hearts are wildly mad,—
  Down at moonlit Eldorado.

The Mulatto's Song

I

Die, you vain but sweet desires!
  Die, you living, burning fires!
I am like a prince of France,—
  Like a prince whose noble sires
Have been robbed of heritage;
  I am phantom derelict,
Drifting on a flaming sea.

II

Everywhere I go, I strive,
  Vainly strive for greater things;
Daisies die, and stars are cold,
  And canary never sings;
Where I go they mock my name,
  Never grant me liberty,
Chance·to breathe and chance to do.

Cora

I

Romance, who sleeps and dreams with me,
　In cup of amaranth and roses, too,
Once more thou stringest melody
　Conceived of cloud and heaven blue;
Once more I look into thy eyes,
　Kissed by the mellow summer moon,
And wonder where my wild heart lies,—
　Wild heart that now is in its noon.

II

Ah, lazy dreamer, where the stars
　Go swimming in the ether deep,
And play a hundred golden bars,
　The sweetest maiden lies asleep
On barge wrought from the snowy cloud;
　And she is Queen, my darling Queen,
My life, my hope, my angel proud,—
　The first this gloomy earth has seen.

III

Romance, didst thou conceive her form,
　Her life, so young and richly sweet,
And place her where the winter storm
　Would cause her tender heart to bleed?

Romance, thou simple, dolting pest,
  Thou mak'st me but an idle child,
A gazer on the charming sex,—
  On Cora—Cora—darling child.

Come Along

I

Come along, mah honey, come along!
Lovin' time's de time tuh sing a song;
Mistuh Moon up daih am lookin' down,
Castin' all de light upon de ground;
Wants tuh make de way ob lub so bright
Dat you hahdly know 'twas day o' night;
Foh de June-time an' de rose am heah,
An' you am mah honey an' mah deah.

II

Come along, mah honey, come along!
Nevah knew dat kissin' was a wrong;
Let me slip mah ahm aroun' yo' wais',
Foh dat am a lovah's right an' place;
Let me sho' yo' how mah heahtstrings beat,
W'en foh you each houah Ah feel a need,
Froo de June-time w'en de rose am heah,
An' you am mah honey an' mah deah.

Malindy

I

De cotton flowah's bloomin' in de fiel',
De sun frum out de dahkness 'gins tuh steal;
De dahkies happy 'mong de wavin' cohn,
Lak sinnahs w'en in God at fust dey's bohn;
Mah sweet Malindy stole away frum wohk,
De dev'lish hoein' Ah begin tuh shuhk;
We's kissin' down behin' de shingle bahn,
De ways ob love we's tryin' hahd tuh lahn.

II

W'en time makes de moon ez soft an' white
Ez snow dat covahs chill Ohio's side;
W'en bleedin' roses dot de grass o' blue,
An' di'monds spahkle in de dew,
Malindy's gwine tuh waih de orange bloom,
An' mahch wid me w'en sounds de weddin'
    chune;
Malindy's gwine tuh be mah honey bride,
An' happy lib fohevah by mah side.

In the Evening

I.

In the evening, love returns,
  Like a wand'rer 'cross the sea;
In the evening, love returns
  With a violet for me;
In the evening, life's a song,
  And the fields are full of green;
All the stars are golden crowns,
  And the eye of God is keen.

II

In the evening, sorrow dies
  With the setting of the sun;
In the evening, joy begins,
  When the course of mirth is done;
In the evening, kisses sweet
  Droop upon the passion vine;
In the evening comes your voice:
  "I am yours, and you are mine."

Dream Song

I

Let me dream a while; the day is done;
   Let me drift away in Charon's barge;
Moonlight pours upon the Isle of Love;
   There the pleasure fairies rove at large;
Mab and sweet Titania are there,
   Oberon and Puck, that rogue of night,
Garbed in wings that dropped from butter-
     flies,
   Ere the sun began to lose its light.

II

There the poets play on golden lyres,
   And the shepherds, with their oaten reeds,
Sailing down the silver stream of song,
   Change to angel flight the lover's deeds;
Like a mystic panorama show,
   All the world of fancy comes to night;
Like a fading panorama show,
   Dances here the minstrel and the sprite.

III

All the world's a dream, but men are mists;
   All this living but a fading dream;
Life is merely night to Heaven's day;
   We are merely grasping for the gleam

44

That, when morning comes in form of
    Death,
Shall be shining on the distant isle,
Clothed in all the splendor of the sun,—
    Clothed in all the splendor of His smile.

When I Die

I

When I die my song shall be,
Crooning of the summer breeze;
When I die my shroud shall be,
Leaves plucked from the maple trees;
On a couch as green as moss
And a bed as soft as down,
I shall sleep and dream my dream
Of a poet's laurel crown.

II

When I die my star shall drop
Singing like a nightingale;
When I die my soul shall rise,
Where the lyre strings never fail;
In the rose my blood shall lie,
In the violet the smile,
And the moonbeams thousand strong,
Past my grave each night shall file.

Mah Mammy

Mah Mammy's haid am whitah dan de snow
Dat falls so lightly on de rivah sho';
Mah Mammy's eyes am tiahed ob dis hyar
    life,
Dat's full ob nuffin' but dahk woe an' strife;
Mah Mammy's face an' hands am shrinkin'
    up,
De fiah ob trubbles dried 'em to a pulp;
But evah night she sits upon de stoop
An' offen do Ah see huh eyelids droop,
W'en Uncle Ephraim plays his banjo song,
De ebenin' froo an' all de nightime long,
Daih's teahs dats sweetah dan de sugahcane,
Daih's teahs dat falls as gently as de rain;
An' mammy sheds 'em when she heahs de
    chune,
Dat's softah dan de moonlight in de June;
Kase w'en ole Uncle Eph an' she war young
Dey went a spahkin' whar de holly's hung,
An' at de sunset time gay Ephraim came,
An' on his banjo praised huh honey name;
But daddy won huh heaht, an' she took him,
An' now w'en all de wohld am cold an' dim,
She laks to heah de banjo ringin' cleah,
She laks to heah de banjo song draw neah.

The Song of the Titanic Victim

I

Water black and briny for my shroud,
Pillow made of seaweed, thick and green,
Couch of coral, pearl, and oyster shell,
Fairer bed no mortal eye hath seen,
And my dirge, the wailing at the bar,
Of the loving ones I left behind,
And my sweetest memory the hour
When I heard the playing of the chimes.

II

I am dreaming all the night-time long;
I am dreaming of a summer land,
While the mermaids swim above my couch,
Singing low a song so sweet and grand,
That I fain would rue the judgment day,
When I must return to whence I came,
That I fain would lie beneath the sea,
Even after Gabriel calls my name.

Kathleen

I

Fair the bogs and hills and dales,
Fair Killarney's mossy vales,
    Ochone! Ochone!
But none looks so fair, I ween,
As my dimpled sweet Kathleen,
    Ochone! Ochone!

II

Ah, the wraithies sing all night
Of her eyes a shinin' bright,
    Ochone! Ochone!
Mary Mother, rest her soul,
Kathleen's purer than the gold,
    Ochone! Ochone!

III

Let the droonin' bagpipes play,
Tunes on this, my weddin' day,
    Ochone! Ochone!
We are one this very e'en
You and I, my dear Kathleen,
    Ochone! Ochone!

The Whisper of the Wind

I

The wind is whispering to the blade of grass,
"I know a land beyond the lily moon,
Beyond the sun, beyond the melting blue
Where every month is but the month of
    June."

II

"And like the morning star that guards the
    East,
Are maidens dwelling in that summer land;
Upon their cheeks Aurora's crimson blush;
Beneath their feet the ocean and the sand."

III

" 'Tis there I go when evening wraps the
    earth
In dusky mantle, and the sun retires;
'Tis there I go and woo the maidens fair
Like minstrel playing on a thousand
    lyres."

IV

"O lovely are the tunes for them I croon
Unlike the harsher note I sing on earth;
And all the giddy stars above come out
And in the spell of music cease their mirth."

The Awakening of Poesy

I

'Tis a joyous day in June,
(Crimson was the midnight moon)
And the lily clothed in white
Opes her eye to dancing light,
As the muse of Nature flies
Down to gaze upon their eyes.
Modest are the daffodils
Growing on bleak Berkshire's hill;
From its cave of ice and snows,
Kissed by every wind that blows,
Leaps eternally the brook
Down into a verdant nook,
Where a youthful dryad sleeps
And the sunlight softly creeps.
Eager for the drowsy bliss
Of a fairy's passion kiss,
From the heart of every rose
Blood of wounded Beauty flows
Deep into the bowels of earth,
Giving to the world the birth
Of a spirit fine and rare,
As the goal of fragrant air.
Swifter than an idle thought

Flies this child that Nature wrought.
(What rings true in earthly name,
She and Beauty are the same)
And the heart of man is warm
When he feels the love day's charm.
Southwind croons soft lullabyes,
Where the blue-eyed pansy lies;
Pan begins to tune his pipe,
For the singing hour is ripe.
Through the world we hear his horn,
"Wake! Sweet Poesy is born,
Sweet, sweet Poesy is born."

Alone

I

The moon came out of depth
   And cried, "Art thou alone?
For I can feel thy grief,
   Poor earth-fed soul, unknown
To those around thy hearth;
The frost-winds moan for thee,
The salt tears fill the sea;
Thy blood is on the reef;
Thy heart is weighed with grief.
   Like thee, I am Alone."

Of the Rose

I

Oh, the wine of the rose is red!
Oh, the wine of the rose is sweet!
And the heart of the rose is love;—
Love who sleeps at the poet's feet,
    In the dewtime.

II

Oh, the breath of the rose is rare!
Oh, the breath of the rose is fine!
And the soul of its perfume comes
Singing sweet to this heart of mine,
    In the dewtime.

III

Oh, the night of the rose is here!
Oh, the night of the rose is long!
And the garden of my love is bright
With the bloom of a passion song,
    In the dewtime.

IV

Oh, the wine of the rose is red!
Oh, the wine of the rose is sweet!
And the heart of the rose is Love;
Love who sleeps at the maiden's feet,
    In the dewtime.

Mammy's Honey Boy

I

Down in Dixie lan' mah boy's asleep,
Many nights foh him Ah's had mah weep.
Wildes' chile Ah's evah raised at all,
Nevah minded once his mammy's call.
Loved de sinnah's pa'f ob flowahs an' smiles,
Gibben me a thousand pains an' trials;
Yet from him Ah'd nevah, nevah paht,
Kase dat boy am all mah achin' heaht.

II

Sleep on, sleep on, precious honey boy,
Sleep on, dreamin' 'bout yo' gals so coy;
Mak' ole Dixie lan' wid laughtah ring,
Pick a banjo chime an' softly sing;
All de wohld am lak de coldes' night,
When mah wand'rin' chile am from mah
        sight;
Mammy's heaht foh you will allus pine,
Sleep on, sleep on, honey boy of mine.

To an Afro-American Maiden

I

Sweet the perfume of an age bygone
When the gods breathed deep in every
 breeze,
Walked beside the sparkle of the sea,
Made their slumber haunt within the trees;
Now no censers swing along the groves
Of the land where swarthy men were brave,
Now the gods have faded as a dream
And dim yesterday lies in her grave.

II

But within the face of one whose race
Dwells exiled throughout this western land,
Comes in fancy all the days long dead
As tho' painted by a master hand;
Rich old Ethiop and Greece are there
In the swarthy skin and dreamy eye,
And the red man of the forest grants
Raven hair and figure tow'ring high.

III

Proud America to nurture one
Who has robbed the ages of their store,
Races three within her bosom strive,

Illustration by Floyd W. Willis

"Races three within her bosom strive,
panting for the sweets of cant and lore;"

Panting for the sweets of cant and lore;
All the world romantic lives in her
With the minstrels and the knights of mail
And the nymphs that dance within the shade,
Journeymen within the dreaming pale.

The Burden Bearer

I

When the owl sits in the tree,
And from out the vapor moon
Quietly descends the night,
Bringing sleep for earthly boon,
I am restless like the leaves
In the tide of summer breeze;
And beside a dream-lulled stream
Long I chant my heart strung pleas.

II

I am lonely through the years
Like a shadow in the vale;
Never dryad's hand touched mine,
Gently soothing anguish wail;
In the gloom where howl the wolves
Long I lie enwrapped in gray;
And my eyes that drip with tears
Gently to my Maker pray.

Richard Byron

I

Brave soul, who through music's maddened
    charm
Made thy world another Paradise,
Let the boasting seraphs round the Throne,
Whilst thy spirit comes to them arise;
For thy lyre the sweetest viol song,
Though on earth as silent as the tomb,
Shall enflame the heavens with its fire
Till the hour that all must hear their doom.

II

Death is sweet reward for him whose toil
Makes a better home for fellow men,
Rest and peace, and crown of honey rose,
Shall the Master to His minstrel send;
And the tune of birds, his hour's delight
In the land where Night is but a name,
And the couch where Pan has gone to dream,
Shall receive at dew his weary frame.

III

We who dwell awhile within this vale,
Hopeless subject to the pangs of pain,
Long to be with thee in Avalon,
Where the life of man is not a chain;

Where the wine is poured from lily cup
And the song of June is always June;
Where the hours are golden like the flame,
Glowing in the crescent of the moon.

Abendlied

I

When the soul goes wand'ring in the night
On a moonbeam from the shrouded sky,
And the body rests beneath the light
Of the stars that in the morning die,
When dewdrop falls 'pon the pressed eyelid,
Sweet is every joy the nightime knows;
And the worries of the day are hid
Where firefly mysteriously glows.

II

When the soul goes wand'ring in the night
Day descends into the silent stream;
From the throne of God the pale moonlight
Shines above as does a joyous gleam;
Spirits of departed hover near
Bringing peace and calm to aching heart;
Spirits of departed hover near,
Singing low a song of ghostly art.

Mine Rachel

I

Mine Rachel iss der Ghetto rose,
Hor lofe for me nobody knows,
Just like I do at Sabbath time,
When I am chanting psalms sublime.
She weaves a praying shawl for me,
And pours me once mine Shabbos tea,
    Dot Rachel von Guttenheim.

II

She call dot pratin' Isidore
Just once a worthless schemin' bore;
She never trade at Cohen's place,
Although he sell der cheapest lace.
And when last night I asked her why,
I see der lovelight in der eye,
    Of Rachel von Guttenheim.

III

So bring a flask of Yiddish wine,
And all der Kosher meat o' mine,
For once I think I spend a lot,
So happy 'cause a prize I got.
No Gentile ever knew a maid,
Dot put der others in der shade,
    Like Rachel von Guttenheim.

Illion

I

I stood at Illion, and looked upon the world,
Beneath me rolled the ocean of my great
   desire,
The yesterdays that drift into a wasted mist,
And future hours that make my soul a living
   fire;
The love that once was mine descends into
   a vale,
Wherein the angels, man, and devil, never
   trod
(So long I laugh! So long I laugh! So
   long I laugh!
That Jesus smiles, and Mary weeps, and I
   know God).

II

Because I loved too well, from Heaven's
   august Throne
An angel brought the key of nature's
   mystery;
Unlocked the beauty of a smiling April
   morn,
Wherein is writ a woman's tragic history,
And led me where stars change to violets,

59

And sunlight pours into the daisy's gleam-
    ing eye,
Until I slept where moonlight drifts into the
    snow,
Where love is young, and clean-souled men
    can never die.

III

From out the depths of Illion a woman rose;
Her garments swept the dawn, her hair out-
    gleamed the sun,
Her eyes were living coals, the testament of
    God,
For God is love, and love is God, and Eve
    their nun;
Within her breast the longing of the age I
    saw
And clasped her! Clasped her! Clasped her
    hard and clasped her long,
And kissed her once, and kissed her twice,
    and kissed her thrice,
And looking in her eyes I sang an endless
    song.

My Mother

I

She is the golden dream that never dies,
The unrestrainéd summer of my days;
Her arms have crooned my wond'ring eyes
    to rest,
When night-breeze round the murmuring
    river plays;
Her hand has guided me where paths are
    rough,
And storms conspire to turn my steps
    astray;
Her soul has ever played the mirror's part
And showed me good there lies in human
    clay.

II

I never know the night when she is near,
Nor tremble at the turning of the tide;
Her name brings music from a thousand
    lyres,
And draws from secret depths my buried
    pride;
I love her as the brook the river loves,
The springtime bud the sap of April moon;
I love her with a love that never dies,
On eve of snow or breath of rosy June.

III

Her hair is not a golden shade nor brown,
Her cheeks are not the flush of summer rose,
But she is statelier than all the queens
Whose splendor in Gallician garden glows;
My Mother o' the dusk, through thee anon
My God has taught me love for all my race;
And never shall the crowning glory dim
Of those who wear the image of thy face.

When I Speak of Jamie

I

When I speak o' Jamie, sunny lass,
A' the bonny bluebells nod their heads,
Clover dances long th' Highland pass,
Water lilies rise from out their beds;
She is a' the world from Glasgow town
To whaur lies me mither's heather down.

II

When I speak o' Jamie, sunny lass,
Storms that blaw and blaw they gang awa',
Know they waul her meltin' smile will last
And will chase Ol' Nick himself awa';
Gin you know her you will die for her,
Ay, will lay you doon and die for her.

The Wanderer

I

I have wandered through the maze of Time,
Through the Valley of the shadow Death,
I have heard the song of nightingale,
And my cheek has felt the rosebud's breath.

II

I have drunk the dew from lily cup,
And have sailed my barge o'er heaven's blue,
But it seems no matter where I go,
I can live with none, my dear, but you.

Let Us Go Away

Let us go away,
    You and I,
On a crimson ray,
    From the sky.
Let us feel the blue
    Soft and clear,
And the golden hue,
    Be so near.
For the morn is fair
    Where stars lie,
Let us two go there,
    You and I.

To the Queen o' the May

To thee, O Queen, the choice of lovely May,
To thee, the sovereign of the ripened spring,
I bring a coronet of daffodils;
A coronet of lilies white as snow,
That hands as soft as purest ermine fur,
Wove while the graces danced and sang
Upon the cloud-tipped peaks of Iduma;
And at the gentle May's request I beg
To place upon thy head this lordly crown
And cry with all the world, Long live the
    Queen!

B. B.

In my sorrows, in my joys,
In my evening, in my morn,
Beulah shall be like the star
That outvied the vaunting moon.
And my weary soul shall drink
Succor!—Succor from her eyes,—
Eyes that tell a strange old tale;
And my arms shall hold her form,—
Delicate as some sweet nymph,
Strayed from out her woodland home.
And when Wyrd shall mold to ash
This poor shell in which I dwell,
We shall rest, one dust in one.

The Vision of Lazarus

Come from the window, Mary, He has gone,
The night is here, and I would tell my tale
Of wondrous sights I saw among the dead,
And music sweeter than the minstrel song,
Of creatures fairer than the noonday sun,
And land where sorrow fades as in a dream.
For I was stretched upon a slab of stone
And laid by thee within a vault of rock,
I never saw thy robes of sombre ash
For I had gone upon the pilgrimage
Of Death, the last long pilgrimage called
    death.
It was a journey o'er the Milky Way,
Far past the golden stars that shine at night,
And o'er a mystic stream, whose waters
    black
Lay slumb'ring in a realm of sunless day,
I glided as a dove who bears sweet words
To some coy maiden by the Galilee,
Until I stood a thousand thousand leagues,
Above the crimson-tinted clouds that drift
As Cleopatra's barge a-down the Nile,
And there I saw a youth unlike the men of
    earth,

All clothed in robes as flimsy as the gauze
That separates the day from eventide.
Whose eye was like the nodding violet
When April weeps upon a grassy slope;
Whose voice came ever soft and low and
    sweet
As when the wind sings me a plaintive song.
"Good Lazarus, I am that Israfel
Who makes the realm of paradise to ring
With melody so wild and clear, the night
And all the stars that light the universe
Glide forth to hear the music of my lute.
To thee I come from Him whose majesty
The thunder and the waterfall have caught
To shew thee all the sights that men may see
When earthly life has run its merry course;
For thou art he who dreamed sweet dreams
Beside the Galilee while others toiled
Athwart the wheel or in the field of corn.
And worthy shalt thou be of Israfel,
And worthy Israfel of thee, my friend."
Thus spake the man of wondrous counte-
    nance
And took me by the hand and led me on
To where the gates of gold like Pyrrhan
    plate

Shine in the splendour of the mystic light;
I heard a chord so grand the thunderstorm
Whose music wakes the slumb'ring souls of
        men
To it was like the faintest ecstasy,
"My choir is chanting praise to God the
        King,"
Said Israfel, and thus the angels sang:—

LAUS JEHOVA

I

Sing to him, ye hosts of Paradise,
Great Jehova rules triumphant now,
Through the works of Lord Emmanuel,
All the erring sons of Adam bow;
When in sylvan vales His name is heard,
Cedar bends in willing suppliance,
Night-breeze croons His praise to all
        the trees
To the river and the running sands.

II

Sing to Him, ye hosts of Paradise,
He has chained the lightning and the
        fire,
He has calmed the spectre of the sea,

He has lifted man from out the mire;
Vaunting Pharaoh is prostrate now,
Jezebel lies reeking in her gore,
All the hearts of men through love and
truth
Upward to His Judgment Seat must
soar.

Like weird enchantment from the Chaldee's
brain
Swung ope the portals, and a perfume sweet
From garden where the Tigris winds her
course,
Enthralled my senses as a man of craft
Beholds a lovely maiden, fit to serve
In Caesar's palace, and with subtlety
Makes her his slave, a piece of chattel flesh.
It was a place so fair that Lebanon,
Whose cedars Venus planted long ago,
Has in her heart an envy of that land;
And Dawn, before her master's chariot
When Love describes the Vale of Paradise
Tints deep her olive cheek with crimson
blush
(If ever death takes me from thee again
May I be there with Israfel and God).

High climbs the vines with grapes so deeply
    red
The harvest moon pales in comparison,
And wine, in which the spirit Youth was
    born,
Flows freely down to where the angels
    quaff;
A river clearer than the crystal ray
Reposes near a bed of hyacinth,
And there on couch with coverlet of rose
Our master singers rest from earthly toil,
And coronets of laurel press their brows,—
The chief reward for pain and suffering;
The singing birds beguile their hours with
    song,
The lilies spring unbidden 'neath their feet,
The breezes croon to them a melody.
And Pain, which once was deemed their
    festive guest,
Lies panting far away, too weak to know
The triumphs and the joys the minstrels
    have.
Among this group reclined an aged man,
His hair and beard as white as virgin snow;
His eyes, which never saw great nature's
    realm,

69

Like eager maiden on her wedding day,—
Awaiting anxiously the coming of her
      swain,—
Grasped fervently the beauty earth denied.
" 'Tis Father Homer; he who sang of Troy,
Of Troy, the land of fable and of song,"
Said Israfel, and to the aged spoke,
"O Father! here is one, sweet Lazarus
Who sings beside the banks of Galilee.
He gave the Son of Man a crust of bread,
A cup to drink, a place to lay his head,
And now that Death has ta'en him from
      below,
God grants that he may look on Paradise."
The Grecian master smiled, and clasped my
      hand,
"To thee, my son, I bid a welcome sweet,
And offer thee a bowl of ruddy wine,
Such nectar none but mighty poets drink.
And I who sang the fall of Ilium,
The wrath and vengeance great Achilles
      wrought,
Wouldst hear a word about the King of
      Kings.
Mayhap his feet are sore and travel bruised,
And Hunger with his tooth is gnawing him,

And all the earth rejects his teachings now
That in the years to come will call Him
   God."
Ah, willingly I quaffed that cup of wine
And told how Jesus comes to Bethany,
And how he preaches here about the love
That shall restore the throne of Israel.
"To us who sing," our Father Homer said,
"The gates are ope, though Christ be yet on
   earth,
This is Elysium, the poets' couch,
And every one who feels the lyric strain
Has caught the fire of God and lives anew,
Though he strew flowers before grim
   Ashtoreth.
Now, when I learned the mystery of God
I wept because no Hector greeted me,
No crafty-tongued Ulysses waited here,
No Hebe poured for me a nectar cup,
And high Olympus with her crown of snow
And mighty deities in Council state
Were vanished like the stars at morning
   time.
A purer heaven thrived than that of Greece,
And those who leapt into a demigod
When hot imagination seized my brain

Were like the mist that droops o'er Ida's
    mount,
Mere vapor rising from an idle dream.
My Aphrodite never looked so fair
As Israfel when chanting praise to God;
Great Juno's wrath was naught to Gabriel's
    voice
When giving message from Jehovah's seat
To wayward clay that lords his fellowmen,
Parnassus where the Muses played and
    danced.
Descended to the humblest garden spot
That flourishes in soft Illyria
When first I gazed upon the cypress grove
Where dwells sweet Israfel and all his choir.
O Lazarus, no wand'ring minstrel's brain
Could bring from fancy such a chimera,
No musing bard, whose eyes were dim with
    time
Could dream of such a land as Paradise."
The old man smiled as when a summer morn
Breaks gently through a gossamer of cloud
And all the cedar and the cypress trees
Their willing branches bent when he was
    done.
Another sate near him, whose harp of gold

Had sounded in the tents of Israel,
His robes were woven from the cloth of Tyre
And golden sandals bound his olive feet
"I am that David, he whose psalms ye sing
When sounds the cymbral in the plains of
    Gad.
My garments, washed of every crimson
    stain,
I am a wearer of the laurel wreath,
My heart as free as when in Bethlehem
I caused the blades of grass to dance with
    glee;
My soul each eventide goes forth with God,
A humble servant to His mystic will;
And in the morning do I wander wide,
Along the cool of every haunt and vale.
There lies a still brook deep in Heaven's
    land
Where milk-white sheep may stray and
    quench their thirst,
And there I nurse my memories of one
I wooed when in the house of lordly Saul.
A virgin like the rose when glides the wind
From out the Southland in the old year's
    noon."

And then a handsome man whose garments
    fell
Across his shoulders like a maiden coy
Whose wrists wore bracelets made of burn-
    ing gold.
Spake, "I am Solomon, who once was king."
I kissed the crystal hand he held to me,
And from my heart there leapt a song of
    praise,
"O sweetest singer in the land of Jude,
The aloes and the pomegranates long
For thee, and nightbreeze sighs when falls
    the dew
Upon thy sepulchre by Jordan's stream
The pensive maid beside the garden wall
Lists eagerly to reading of thy Song.
For first was thou to chant the joys of love,
The dew of passion kiss upon the lips,
The heaving of the soul within the breast,
The bed of leaves beside dark Kedar's tent."
And then I bade the singing ones farewell,
"Oh, come again, sweet Lazarus," cried they,
"And fair and soft and cool thy rest shalt be,
Thy food and fare the sweetest honeycomb,
Thy drink, the wine distilled from beams of
    moon,"

From thence good Israfel and I fared forth
To where the stream of life sleeps in a wood
Beneath the glory of the throne of God;
And when I gazed upon the crystal sheet
Lo! like the quick phantasma of a dream.
The future danced before my wond'ring
        eyes,
I saw the Master nailed upon the cross,
The price the world must pay for holiness.
I felt a faith so new and strange the veil
Was torn asunder, and the pillars fell.
"Nay, shudder not," said Israfel, " 'Tis writ
The Lamb of God must die to save the
        world."
Methought I fell a thousand thousand miles
Beneath the all-consuming fire of earth
Into a region void of light and peace,
Where Conscience broods with lash of
        scorpion
And raven shrieks the nameless deeds of
        men;
Where souls lie bare upon a mossy rock
And impish creatures prod their backs with
        prongs;
Where nothing comes into the anxious ear

Save moanings of the spirits Conscience
    lashed.
'Twas then the pallor came upon me thick
And to my angel friend I cried, "Sweet one,
This mystery is pricking ope my wounds,
Let me ascend to where the air comes forth
As goodly as the lily in the spring."
From out a cave I heard a trembling voice,
"Good Lazarus, art thou among the damned,
The wretched and the cursèd seed of man?
Or art thou come to cool the parching
    tongue
Of him who once was King of Macedon,
Great Alexander, one whose name was law
From sunny isle in Greece to farthest Ind.
The pampered idol of a subdued world.
Between the flowing of a bowl of wine
And fever of a woman's honeyed kiss
Came I into this world of gloom and pain.
Far better death upon a bloody spear
Than such an end to earthly strife and woe.
Far better Poverty should gnaw the bone
Than dwell in anguish here and deep despair.
Go forth, sweet soul, to where the sunlight
    pours
And seek the one who knows Elysium,

For he will lead thee to where the fields are
    green
And founts of water cool the burning
    tongue."
Quick from a crater red with belching fire
A hornéd form bestrided upper Hell;
His eye was dark and pierced me like a bolt
Of lightning in an angry summer storm;
Like thunder in the cave of Sinai
He roared and all the depths of Sheol shook.
"Thou, Israfel, who spoiled my chance to
    rule,
When I rebelled against Jehovah's throne
Thou traitor knave, thou fawning piece of
    air,
Thou whining dog whose music is thy bite;
Wouldst thou presume to walk this realm
    of mine
With one who housed and fed the Son of
    God?
'Tis mine, this piece of clay thou bringest
    here;
'Tis mine by primal right bestowed through
    Eve.
No golden Eden nor bright Paradise
For any sprung from sinful Adam's loins,

And I proclaim that he shall not escape
Though all the force of God oppose my
    aim!"
The angel trembled not, but stood his
    ground.
"Base spirit, ruler of the evil heart,
The destiny of Lazarus is where
The soul of Beauty is a god indeed;
Too base for intellect akin to His
The Godhead deems the home of Lucifer,
We merely come to gaze upon thy work
To pass away eternal idle hours.
But if thou dreamest that this poet's soul
Belongs to thee with all thy torturing
Then Israfel will wage a war with thee
Until the pillars of the universe
Go tumbling down into the Lake Chaos."
Then Satan stooped and swung a mighty
    stone,
So huge the fabled Cyclop was mere mite,
Mere mite, and swaying, plunged it toward
    Israfel,
Who, quicker than the breeze outstrips the
    stream,
Avoided it, and smiled to see it fall
So gently to the ground before his feet,

A better weapon had this singing soul
The mystery and sweetness of his voice,
Which loosened charms the roaring ele-
    ments,
He sang a song so weird and strange and
    grand,
The devil cowered, wond'ring at the spell
And thus a seeming age they fought o'er me
Who crouched behind a boulder, weak with
    fear
And neither fiend nor angel won the day,
Tho' Satan stood upon the prostrate form
Of Israfel, and raised his burning sword;
And then methought the vision died away
Into the light of glorious daytime.
And Satan blinded by the angel spell
Seized me, and tore to shreds my holiness.
Poor Israfel when this he saw wept loud
But God above had turned His willing ear;
I heard the Master's voice like thunder roll,
Into my dreaming, "Lazarus, come forth."

Afterword.

And now my chord is silent. The night has come upon the land, and I fain would rest. Perhaps I have pleased thee, perhaps I have not. There are many minstrels, O my King the Reader, and I am the humblest in all thy realm. May our parting be
                    Auf Wiedersehen!
                        THE SINGER.